Goodbye Old, Hello *Bold*

OTHER BOOKS BY J.J. HUBAL

A Week at the Beach: 100 Life-Changing Things You Can Do by the Seashore (2003)

Living with Your Higher Power: A Workbook for Steps 1-3 (2021)

Living with Your Higher Power: A Workbook for Steps 4-7 (2021)

Living with Your Higher Power: A Workbook for Steps 8-12 (2021)

Goodbye Old, Hello *Bold*

A JOYFUL LEAP INTO A WORLD OF NEW POSSIBILITIES AS WE AGE

WRITTEN AND DRAWN BY
J.J. HUBAL

MIAMI

For permission requests, please contact the publisher at:
Mango Publishing Group
5966 South Dixie Highway, Suite 300
Miami, FL 33143
info@mango.bz

For special orders, quantity sales, course adoptions and corporate
sales, please email the publisher at sales@mango.bz. For trade
and wholesale sales, please contact Ingram Publisher Services at
customer.service@ingramcontent.com or +1.800.509.4887.

Goodbye Old, Hello Bold: A Joyful Leap into a World of New
Possibilities as We Age

Library of Congress Cataloging-in-Publication number: 2024946232
ISBN: (print) 978-1-68481-703-0, (ebook) 978-1-68481-704-7
BISAC category code: SEL005000, SELF-HELP / Aging

To Jim

I truly don't understand how this happened. *This.*

One day I was young,

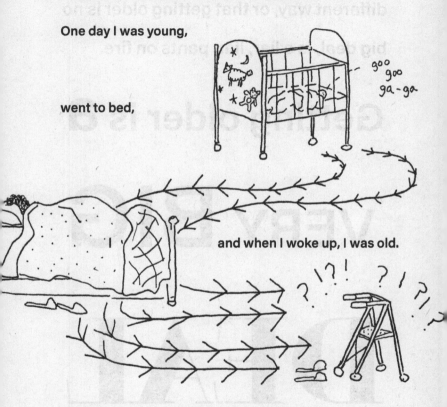

went to bed,

and when I woke up, I was old.

That's how it happens; without warning you're

THERE

Anyone who says it happens in a different way, or that getting older is no big deal, is a liar, liar, pants on fire.

Getting older is a

VERY BIG

DEAL

To prove my point, remember.

Think back to a time before ALL OF IT

happened—a time before

REALITY **had to be faced.**

Back when getting old was a **distant star** and *POSSIBILITY* was everywhere.

The world is your oyster.

Back when we believed the clichés about life were

real, and our future was only a matter of hard

work and positive thinking.

First comes love, then comes marriage, then comes baby. in a baby carriage.

Success is 99% perspiration.

Education is the Key to everything!

Back when we didn't realize that the

only way to have a different NOW is to have been

born as that *other person*—

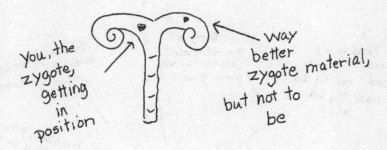

You, the zygote, getting in position

Way better zygote material, but not to be

the one who lived a life that turned out so much better
than the one we got stuck with.

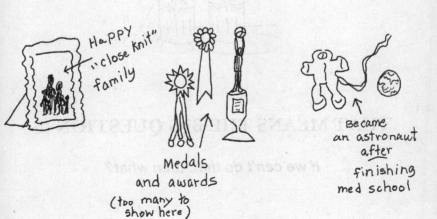

HaPPY "close knit" family

Medals and awards
(too many to show here)

Became an astronaut after finishing med school

The person born as the imagined us, who had

THE LIFE WE ALWAYS WANTED

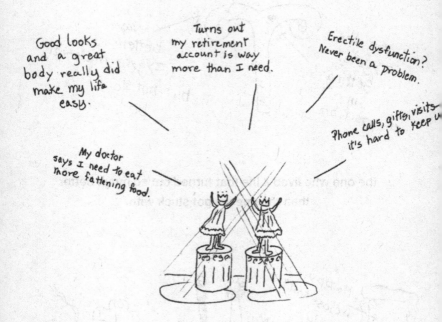

THAT MEANS THE BIG QUESTION IS

If we can't do that, then what?

Bungee jumping in Nepal?

Rolling up in a fetal position to wait for the

Grim Reaper?

Or something in between?

This book is about exactly that—

T H E   S O M E T H I N G   I N   B E T W E E N

the what's *still* possible.

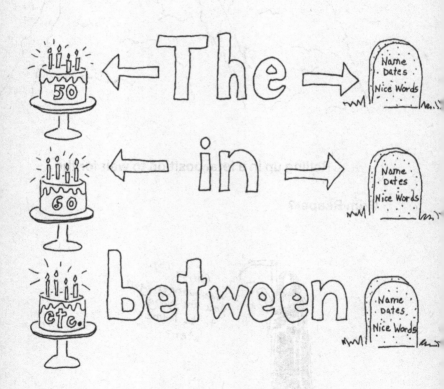

But

Where *do* we start?

We start where all

great journeys begin,

with a leap...

Away from our comfy chair **in front of the TV**

Or wandering aimlessly around *THE MALL,*

Or wandering aimlessly online, clicking from link to link

Away from people who want us to think

exactly **like they do—who think their way is**

THE   ONLY   WAY

Away from people who live small fearful lives.

Planes can Crash, you Know besides I heard food in those other countries is weird and might even Kill you which is why I'm staying right here in my own back yard of the house I grew up in which is safe and sound

Buying a house is such a big commitment and so is getting married and getting a pet even though I would love to have a dog it is out of the question

I've always wanted to dance, live in an apartment, run a company, have children, move to Costa Rica, roller blade but but but but but but but but

I don't like tests so I never got a driver's licence, a college degree, a black belt in Karate, a promotion, became a chef, a nurse, a pilot, a life guard, or had a real physical, and so far so good in my opinion

Exact same hair-do since high school Why mess with a good thing plus I'd have to change beauticians now you're talking crazy she would be very upset with me if she found out and I won't

**And the drama of people who need rescuing—again,
and again,   and**

a g a i n   and

a
   g
a   i
   n

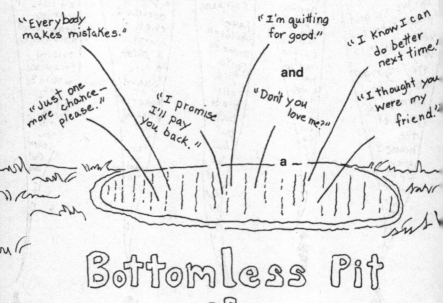

"Everybody
makes mistakes."

"I'm quitting
for good."

"I know I can
do better
next time!"

and

"Just one
more chance—
please."

"I promise
I'll pay
you back."

"Don't you
love me?"

"I thought you
were my
friend."

a

Away from anything and anyone that is taking up valuable real estate in our hearts or minds or schedules or homes or to-do lists to make room for things and people and places that are a better fit for our lives *right now.*

*This exact second.

*This exact day.

*This exact life.

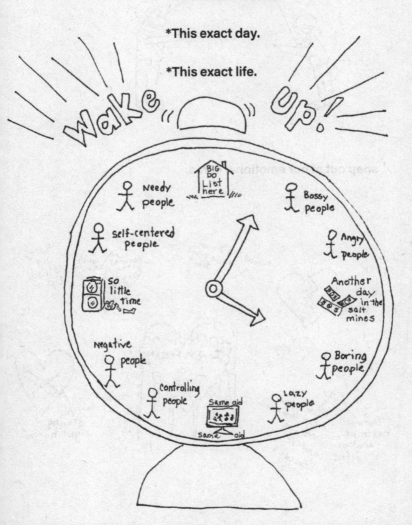

We'll stop fighting tiny wars with no winners,

snap out of our emotional coma,

and run from **THE GREAT NEVER-**

ENDING THING

"Pump as much money
into me as you want,
but I'll never
really run right."

"Pay for my tuition,
my apartment, my car,
my wedding, my credit
card and I still won't
be able to live
on my own."

"Spray, pull, and dig to your heart's
content — there's lots more
where we came from."

We'll fly out of reach of our corner office with a view, or the small space in a dismal dead-end job that sucks our soul dry, away from anything we do for money—even boatloads of money—that stopped making sense a long time ago.

"For the life of me, I can't remember why I thought I needed this much."

We won't look back at ideas that are

nevereverneverever going to come to fruition,

and dreams that will **nevereverneverever**

come true.

Glide past things that remind us of people that are

NOT COMING BACK

Our first apartment

where our best friends lived

our favorite coffee shop

street where we used to live

Our bench

Old photo albums

more here plus videos and nostalgic music

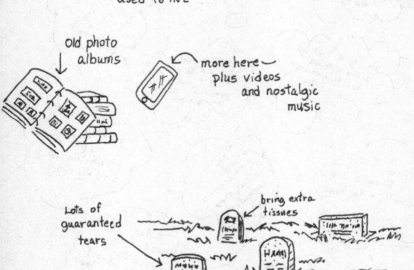

Lots of guaranteed tears

bring extra tissues

even the person we

USED TO BE

"I was so skinny they called me 'toothpick'."

"People always came to me for advice."

"I can still hear the roar of the crowd."

"I was the best mom ever."

"My hair was legendary."

Get away from opportunities that

AREN'T GOING TO KNOCK TWICE

no matter how patiently we wait.

Or the choices we *had*:

★ **investments that might have made millions**

★ **the family we always wanted**

★ **the right turn on the career path highway**

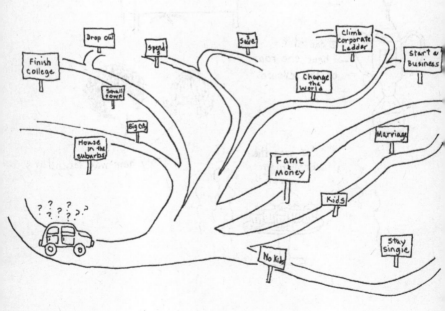

Whatever worn-out shoe fits, take it off and

*Let It Go**

*It's over

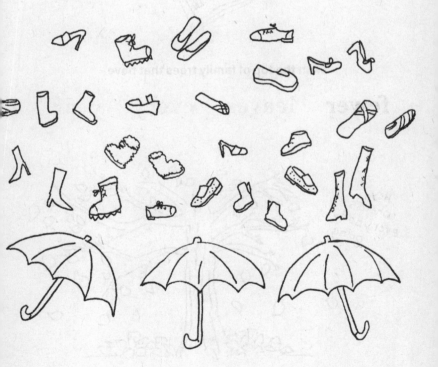

Fly away from **old habits** like reading the obituaries to

"see if we're still on the right side of the grass."

Skim the top of family trees that have

fewer   leaves   every   year.

We'll let books that don't interest us remain unread,

even if someone gave it to us for "your own good,"

or because they "know you'll love this."

We'll

z—o—o—m p—a—s—t

predictable family gatherings

and soar above (a)lone-ly marriage(s)

"Forty years together and
    he's not sure it's really
        working for him."

and WORN-OUT PARTNERSHIPS

"I want my turn."   "what's
                                a 'turn'?"

and lost loves that need to stay that way.

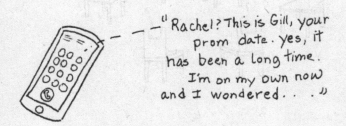

"Rachel? This is Gill, your
    prom date. yes, it
has been a long time.
    I'm on my own now
and I wondered. . . ."

We'll go   *missing*   from groups that

no longer serve us,

or ones that are just plain wrong.

And leave *lopsided friendships,*

even if they're lifelong.

We'll stop waiting by the computer or phone for that

certain best ever perfect soulmate gotta have

SOMEONE

to contact us.

Or worse yet, send out one more cat video that will

give you a chuckle.

"My antics are
sure-fire
friend makers."

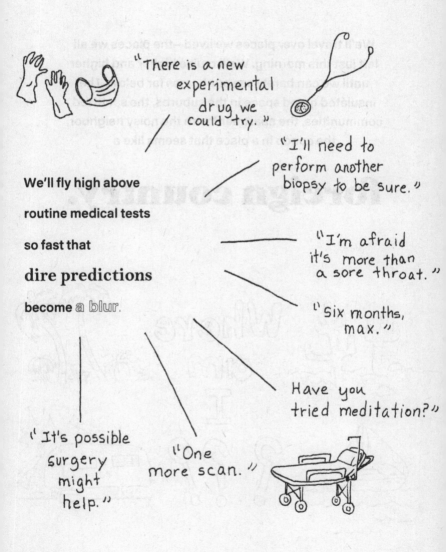

"There is a new experimental drug we could try."

"I'll need to perform another biopsy to be sure."

We'll fly high above

routine medical tests

so fast that

dire predictions

become a blur.

"I'm afraid it's more than a sore throat."

"Six months, max."

"Have you tried meditation?"

"It's possible surgery might help."

"One more scan."

We'll travel over places we lived—the places we all left just this morning. We'll cruise higher and higher until we can barely see our homes far below. The insulated gated space in the suburbs, the sanitized communities, the apartment with the noisy neighbor, the condo in a place that seems like a

foreign country.

And the stuff **STUFF** Stuff *STUFF* stuff *stuff*

AND

more&more&more&more&more&

more&**more**&**more**

STUFF that fills every nook and cranny.

"Trust me, the kids don't want us."

"They called me crap — hurtful."

"Toss me and you'll regret it."

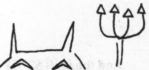

We'll fly so high, in fact, we can no longer see our dirtiest of

dirty little secrets—**A STORAGE UNIT**

for all the pieces of the past we might use

S O M E

D A Y

S O M E O N E

M I G H T N E E D

T H I S A N D W E W I L L B E

READY READY READY READY READY READY READY

Speed up! Go faster *and faster* until none of us
can hear the voices of all the people who need us to
stay exactly

As   We   Are

until we can't feel any of our **burdens**—

not even the ones that we chose.

Beautiful to look at, but tons of work.

Fabulous view, but four flights of stairs is a nightmare

Unconditional love, but. . .

Not even our

BIGGEST

MISTAKES

We're lighter now—uncluttered mind, open heart, empty calendar—and begin to F L O A T; we are

FLOATING   FLOATING   FLOATING

A W A Y

This minute

OLD doesn't matter—

we're off to think some possible thoughts and see

new opportunities, or bits and pieces of old dreams that might

still have a chance.

grow support travel hug learn contact
love see do help build go
share change make promise teach try
eat create cook
touch

We're going to explore

the spaces in our world with

fresh new eyes.

We're going to try new things, or maybe revisit some old ones—even with **UNCOOPERATIVE** body parts.

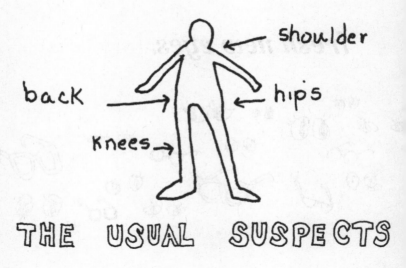

THE   USUAL   SUSPECTS

We're going to **STOP THINKING SO MUCH!**

and start saying YES OK YOUBET

ICAN IWILL IDLOVETO

LETSGO SOUNDSGREAT

EXCITING ICANTWAIT OKEY

DOKEY WHENDOWESTART

IMREADY WOOHOO COUNTMEIN

YESYESYESYESYESYES

YESYESYESYESYESYESYES…

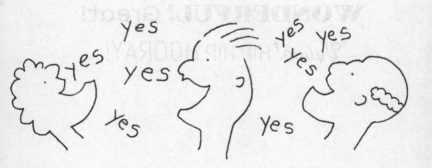

BUT

Everybody knows life deals us all different cards. Some of us have lost everyone and everything; some of us have people and money. We know the playing field gets more uneven every minute we're alive. *Saying* yes might be easy; *doing* is quite another matter.

And what about those of us who have nothing left on our plate, or have no plate at all? If that's you…

WONDERFUL! Great!
Yahoo! HIP HIP HOORAY!

That means the rest of your life is a blank slate,

and in spite of the doomsday voices in our head shouting

otherwise

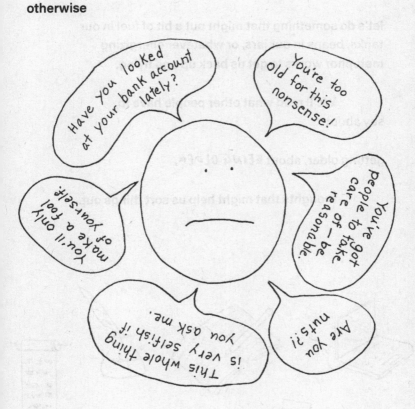

there are still great things—

possible new things—left to do.

first

Let's take a break—

let's do something that might put a bit of fuel in our tanks, beans in our jars, or whatever energizing metaphor works to get us back up and flying.

We'll read what other people have to say about

getting older, about BEiNG OLDER,

thoughts that might help us sort things out.

QUOTES AHEAD ➡

Quotes Ahead ➡

QUOTES AHEAD ➡

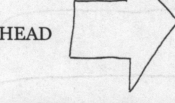

"Old is what you get if you're lucky."

—Elizabeth Somer, *Age-Proof Your Body*

"The older I get, the more clearly I remember things that never happened."

—Mark Twain

"There is still no cure for the common birthday."

—John Glenn

"As long as we keep comparing ourselves to a younger, better self... we shortchange the possibilities for becoming an older, wiser one."

—Henry Simmons and Jane Wilson, *Soulful Aging*

"Experience has taught me you cannot value dreams according to their odds of coming true."
—Sonia Sotomayor

"If I'd known I was going to live this long, I'd have taken better care of myself."

—Eubie Blake on his ninety-sixth birthday

"I wish I were what I was when I wished I were what I am."

—Tongue Twister

"Remembering that I'll be dead soon is the most important tool I've ever encountered to help me make the big choices in life."

—Steve Jobs

"Confident people don't think about how old they are; they think about what they can accomplish with the time they have left."

—Joyce Meyer, *Power Thoughts Devotional*

"While there's life, there is hope."

—Stephen Hawking

"It is not impossibilities which fill us with the deepest despair, but possibilities which we have failed to realize."

—Robert Mallett, Deputy Secretary, USDC

"The best time to plant a tree is twenty years ago. The next best time is now."

—Anonymous

"When we're young, we have the advantage of thinking we're going to live forever. When we're older, we have the advantage of knowing we won't." —Katherine Nouri Hughes, author of *The Mapmaker's Daughter*

"The most important thing in life is, if you have a dream—I mean a real good dream, follow it." —Evil Knievel

"One of the best things about my life now is having the time and space to finish relationships I ended twenty years ago." —Laura Davis, *I Thought We'd Never Speak Again*

"Let's remember: people getting older is not a crisis; it's a blessing." —Ai-jen Poo, *The Age of Dignity*

"I don't know how to act my age;
I've never been this old before."

—Saying on a T-shirt

"There is evidence all over the place that many of us
are aging amazingly well."

—Marianne Kilkenny, *Your Quest for Home*

"Sometimes, looking back, we see that only
by letting go were we able to move on to new
adventures, new insights and satisfactions."

—Martha Hickman,
Healing After Loss

"If you want to live to a hundred or older,
you can't just sit around waiting for it to happen.
You have to get up each
day and go after it." —George Burns

"I am like a forest that has more than once been cut down. The shoots are livelier than ever."
—Victor Hugo

"One of the things that has helped me... is not how long am I going to live, but how much can I do while living."
—George Washington Carver

"If old age can be an ascension, it is at the same time a letting go."
—May Sarton, *At Seventy*

"We will be known forever by the tracks we leave."
—Dakota Indian Proverb

That's lots of food for thought.

Now we're ready to consider the plate itself, your plate—*the one that holds the rest of your life*:

Who's left on it? Or who would we like to invite on board? Where is it, or where do we want it to be, to live the best chapter yet—the ONLY chapter left to be written?

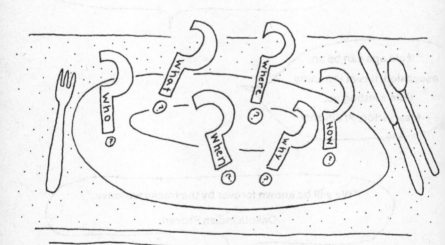

We're so much lighter now that we're

A W A Y **and**

F L O A T I N G

F L O A T I N G to see

if there are any crumbs of a dream that might still
come true, or an idea that is even plausible—or
remotely doable, or has a rat's chance in hell.

Are there any bits of our hoped for life

that might *still* be possible?

We're F L O A T I N G to find out,

F L O A T I N G to figure out,

F L O A T I N G to see for ourselves,

exactly what's...

NEXT

NEXT is anything that works—

for YOU.

Right now

And from

Here

On in

From here

To whatever's

NEXT: *adverb*

1.   **on the first or soonest occasion after the present; immediately afterwards.** "He wondered what would happen next."

As in *Oh, no! What (dread, fear, anxiety, nail-biting) next?*

OR

As in *What (hope, excitement, eager, handclapping) next?*

OR

A sprinkling of each?

OR

Maybe you're one of those people who has loads of great ideas waiting to be hatched (*oh, lucky you*),

I'm going to buy a motorcycle, shave my head, get a cat, join a commune, call my sister, sail around the world, take karate classes, hug my boss, write a novel, learn to yodel, kick my kids out, fall in love, run a motel, learn to tango, build a treehouse, exercise, get *another* cat, have my tattoos removed, wear flip-flops with a suit, go back to school, stop texting, write poetry, learn to swim, ask for a raise, buy a sheep farm, collect rocks, move to another country, get a face lift

But most of us do not. We need help help help help help help help me please I've got no ideas whatsoever help help help help get me started help help help help help I don't know where to begin help help help help it's been a long time since I thought about myself help me do it help help help help help help I'm all ears help help help help my last good idea didn't work out help help help help help help help help help help help help help help help help help help help help help

I've got nothing.

THAT'S WHY SOME OF US MAY NEED A

CHEAT SHEET of IDEAS stepping-stones that may

work, or not, that others have done, or nobody has ever

done, that can get the stuck unstuck, something to try,

to tweak, to move forward, pick and choose, ignore, get

inspired, get bored, but at the very least

GET GOING!

Get a move on!

Get the LEAD OUT!

Here you go...

CiRCLE ANYTHiNG THAT RESONATES
AT ALL—NO ONE'S WATCHiNG:

Quit your job Get a job Play in a band Start a
    B&B Invent something Pay off your debt
Pay off someone else's debt Tap dance Join the
    Peace Corps Explore a cave Live in an RV Live off
the grid Uncover your family secrets
    Run for political office Spend some of your nest
egg Build a tiny house Interview someone
    Learn another language Make something and sell
it Volunteer Make a video about your life Become a
consultant Use Zoom Travel for fun
    Call someone in your family who hurt you Learn to
drive Take a road trip without a map Vegetate
Track down a lost love Give your money away to
    strangers Get married Go to therapy Break up
Hook up Start a retirement account Say
    something nice to someone you can't stand Ask for
help Reconnect with a hobby Schedule a
    cruise Mentor someone Work at a day care
and realize **THERE'S MANY MANY
MANY MANY MORE...**

RIGHT HERE: Teach someone something
Scream Donate your stuff Have more sex
Stop buying more stuff Join a theater group
Polish your toenails Take someone out of your
will Stop wearing neckties Take lessons for
anything you're not good at Live without a car
Rent out something you own Give a speech Sing
Run a race Change your place of worship
Empty a closet Sky dive Sleep in a tent Let your
hair go natural Track down old friends Plan a
party Create an online group Try couples
counseling Travel with strangers Join a co-op
Save a whale Save your neighborhood Save face
Write a will Tell the truth Wear bright colors Write
a book Eat better food Eat more junk
Move to an apartment Start a blog Organize a
reunion Buy a sensible car Change your mind
Start a group Meet with a life coach Walk out
your door Find new friends who are nothing like
you Surprise someone Play a game Join a sports
team Coach a sports team Plant something
Eat in a restaurant where nothing looks familiar
Invite someone to move in OR...

kick someone out Travel somewhere scary Walk
        to everything Get a power chair and use it
Move your body Build furniture Take out a
        restraining order Snorkel Help someone who
doesn't expect it Compliment everyone you meet
        Cry in public Journal Consider co-housing
Adopt new relatives Clean up your street Stop
        looking at old photos and videos Ignore emails
Celebrate without drinking Sleep in a hammock
        Grow a ponytail Set up a scholarship Plant
things you can eat Provide shelter for people or
        animals Invite people into your home Dress for
comfort Reel in a person who has drifted away
        Move somewhere that feeds your soul
Redecorate your space Live on an island Ride a
        horse Finish your education Find a business
partner Be with people who love you back
        Toss your to-do list Become a "Golden Girl" Wear
things that make you feel cool Climb a mountain
        Join a drumming circle Renew your vows Trade
in your minivan Listen to an opera Listen to the
        Grand Ol' Opry Quit kidding yourself House swap
Sponsor a fundraising event Misbehave

And then maybe write your brother
Be a stand-up comic Couch surf around the world
Hold hands Stop swearing Ride a bike in the
snow Invest money Work part-time Weep
uncontrollably Laugh like a hyena Camp with a
child Publish your life story (or someone else's)
Dye your hair purple Put a ramp on your house
Rent (or rent out) a garden space Be an oddball
Tour a tiny town Write your own obituary Flirt
Trade something you do for free rent Trade
something you do for free travel Walk in a
cemetery Apologize Send someone to college
Collect eccentric friends Serve on a board Go
diving Trace your ancestry Fly a drone Wear
high heels Wear cowboy boots Hire help
Start being a "real" parent Celebrate for no reason
Go somewhere you think you shouldn't be Get
new knees Organize your garage Walk slower
Paint a mural Visit an obscure museum Sponsor a
senior animal Move closer to friends Make
yourself indispensable Learn to read lips Wear a
candy mustache Drink great coffee **Sell your**

business **Keep going and** Sell your
house Sell your skills Ride an access bus Go
somewhere else Carry a business card Donate
time Job share Carpool Come to your senses
Punch a pillow Take a train anywhere Sleep naked
Comfort a child Paint a wall something other
than white Take up kickboxing Stop talking
Start a business in your home Wake up Do chair
yoga or television yoga or online yoga or friend yoga
Babysit House sit Pet sit Plant sit Quit caring
what your kids will say Quit caring what the
neighbors will think Make new traditions Open
a savings account Make amends with someone
you've hurt Direct a play Plant trees in a forest,
or a park, or your own backyard Move in
with relatives Date "again" Cancel season's
tickets Invite strangers to a party Go to a quirky
meeting Smile whether you mean it or not Get
your teeth fixed Celebrate "the holidays"
when you feel like it Stop pretending to like
football Hang artwork you created Follow your
doctor's orders and **Most of all, know**

the list of possibilities goes to

INFINITY

And this is the last of it—

YOU have to take it from here.

★ **Meditate**

★ **Pray**

★ **Be silent**

★ **Think**

And **DREAM DREAM DREAM**

HOWEVER,

all the ideas in the whole world won't help at all
unless you pass this test:

At what age should you STOP

caring what other people think?

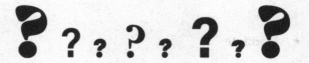

Answer:_____

(write your age here)

YOU PASSED WITH FLYING COLORS
and can start right...

Now nownownownownow

nownow NOW

NOW now now now

NOW

Now NOW

now now now

NOW YOU CAN CREATE, CAN PICK AND CHOOSE,

CAN ERASE AND START OVER AS MANY TIMES AS YOU

WANT. IT'S YOUR LIFE AND YOUR FUTURE SO HAVE AT IT.

YOU'RE GOING TO...

...make Three Lists:

1. Old ideas (remember, explore, revisit, salvage, repurpose, enhance, expand, redo, fix, alter, update, renovate, resurrect)

2. New ideas (dream, read, listen, watch, imagine, open your eyes and ears and life and future and attention to new possibilities)

3. RADICAL iDEAS

(WOWOWOWOWOWOWOWOWOWOWOWOWOWOW
WOWOWOWOWOWOWOWOWOWOWOWOWOW
WOWYOURSELF)

REMEMBER

One person's Old Idea

may be another person's RADICAL one—

or vice versa.

What you put on your

lists is your call

100%

None of anyone's beeswax →

Keep out!!

All trespassers will be very sorry.

Nobody asked for your "input."

LIST NUMBER ONE: Old ideas, or people, or places, or things that might deserve another look.

LIST NUMBER TWO: New ideas, people, places, or things that could be worth trying.

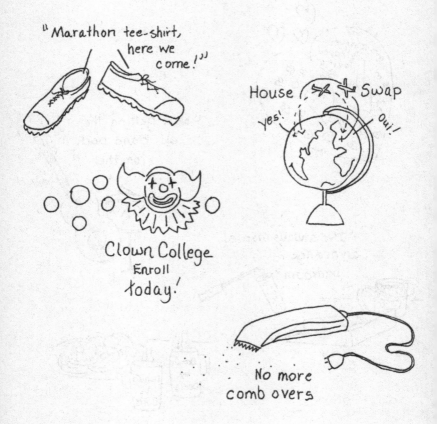

LIST NUMBER THREE: RADICAL iDEAS, OR PEOPLE, OR PLACES, OR THINGS THAT WILL BLOW YOUR MIND, AND MAYBE A FEW OTHER PEOPLE'S MINDS AS WELL.

How hard can it be to raise your own food?

You love kids; we need parents. It's a win-win.

No business suits out here.

Then you'll use your lists to create

Your Chart of Possibilities

here's how...

	People	**Place**	**Things**
Old Ideas	THESE	ARE	THE
New Ideas	SQUARES	WHERE	YOU
Radical Ideas	WILL	WRITE	IDEAS

Your Chart of Possibilities

Here's a sample:

	People	Place	Things
Old Ideas	Go to my class reunion	Volunteer at the zoo	Take my tuba out of storage
New Ideas	Apologize to my neighbor	Rent out spare bedroom	Start wearing a medical alert necklace
Radical Ideas	Sign up for online dating	Bike around Ireland	Sell my car

And here's another sample:

	People	Place	Things
Old ideas	Find a doctor who listens	Plant a container garden	Wear a Kilt
New ideas	Host a block party	Take a cooking class in Paris	Study boat making
Radical ideas	Join a ukulele band	Live in a lighthouse	Buy a bouncy castle

Now it's your turn. Don't think too hard—write!

	People	Place	Things
Old Ideas			
New Ideas			
Radical Ideas			

Your Chart of Possibilities

If you like, keep on writing.

	People	Place	Things
Old Ideas			
New Ideas			
Radical Ideas			

Your Chart of Possibilities

Got more? Go for it!

	People	**Place**	**Things**
Old Ideas			
New Ideas			
Radical Ideas			

Your Chart of Possibilities

Perhaps your style is **no chart at all** because you have your own way of doing **THIS SORT OF THINKING** that works better for you.

Of course, like all good things, no matter what you decide, your lists of possibilities will always be subject to change (or let's hope so), and maybe even more change than you bargained for, so be ready for it.

CHANGE

Change is everywhere all the time

c. h. a. n. g. e.   is   GOOD

AND EVEN IF IT ISN'T

ALWAYS GOOD

you can't avoid it so

DON'T BE SURPRISED WHEN IT HAPPENS
BECAUSE IT MEANS YOU'RE ON TO SOMETHING

THE NEXT STEP IS TO look over your ideas and pick one that catches your attention. Circle it. That idea is your target.

Even if your target is a very big idea, consider it in very, very small, miniscule even, ways. Think of anything you can do that's **within your reach right now** to move in its direction.

You're ready to **start planning** very, very small steps—baby steps—to make it happen. Even if they lead to nothing much, take one step and then another and another and another and another put one foot in front of the other and keep going.

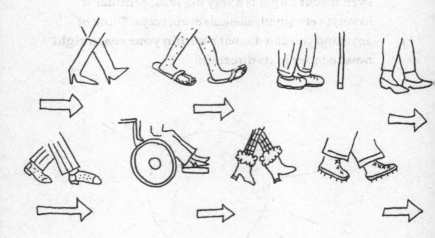

Stepping is the important part even if it's only in the *direction* of things that you already know bring joy or pleasure or hope, or even the hope of joy or pleasure or

hope.

STEP STEP STEP STEP STEP STEP STEP STEP STEP STEP STEP STEP

If you notice you like what you're doing (step step step),

do it for a while.

If you discover you love what you're doing (Step Step Step),

do it longer.

If you start to feel passionate about it (STEP STEP STEP),

do it as long as you like.

Taking steps will tell you in no uncertain terms

which small idea

needs to be much,

much,

B. I. G. G. E. R.

Like this

Step 1

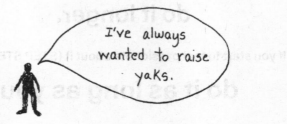

Step 2

Step 3

Step 4

Step 5

Encouraging Testimonial

And it goes without saying:

START OVER AND OVER AND OVER AND OVER AGAIN

as many times as it takes

to find something that fits.

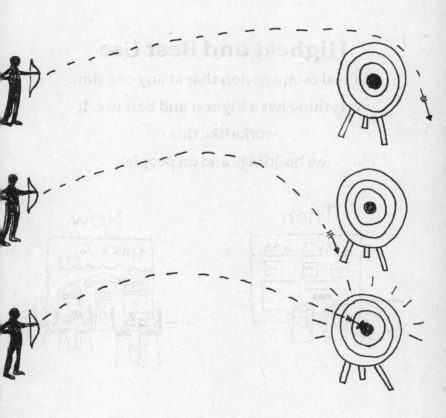

Make a plan that helps create the

HIGHEST AND BEST YOU

at this age, with those hips, and all the

many problems that come with the whole

"getting older" thing.

Highest and Best Use

is a real estate notion that at any one time

everything has a highest and best use. It

works like this

(on buildings and on people):

And at some point you will be in a place many people have been before. You're thinking new thoughts and seeing new possibilities.

You're excited!

The hard part will be going back to the RIGHT NOW—

your house

your people

your schedule

your friends

your gathering places

your responsibilities

your choices

your plans

your promises

your stuff.

They are all right where you left them, and they have

no idea you've been SOMEWHERE ELSE.

BUT *you will know.*

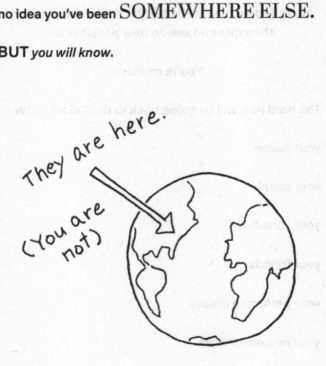

They are here.

(You are not)

And more than that, you know life from now on

will be different because you are *different.*

That means...

You can be the person you imagined.

- ★ brave

- ★ fun

- ★ energetic

- ★ creative

- ★ affectionate

- ★ successful

- ★ healthy

- ★ adventurous

★ calm

★ sexy

★ unpredictable

★ and anything else

★ you've ever

★ wanted to

★ be

Doubt it?   Worried?   Skeptical?

Ready to forget the whole thing?

Let me introduce you to some of the millions

of people who have taken a journey exactly

like the one you've been on.

They took their whims, old dreams, and

wild ideas and made fresh starts and

new connections

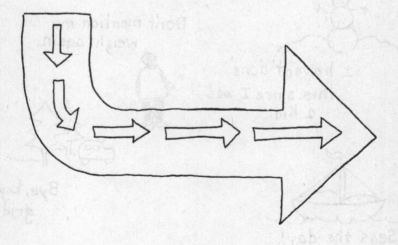

Get down boogie oogie oogie!

This is museum quality.

Because I like yurts, that's why.

I haven't done this since I was a kid.

Don't mention my weight again.

Bye, bye gridloc

Seas the day!

They wrote new clichés to believe in,

   and reclaimed a few old ones.

They DISCOVERED lots loads a whole

bunch more than they thought existed oodles

of wonderful exciting interesting motivating

energizing rejuvenating opportunities choices

magic moments forgotten dreams surprises thrills

adventures peaceful silences options affection

enlightenment deep satisfaction inspiring places

touch love serendipity meaningful conversation

ALL STILL POSSIBLE

The time is here. It's your turn.

All you have to do is

LET   GO   AND   FALL

Fall through space.

Fall till you land on solid ground.

Fall till you land...

exactly where you need to be,

with people who are the best possible match for you,

and do precisely the thing only you can do.

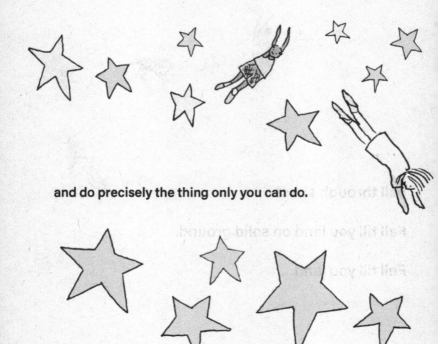

a   n   d

live

that

way...

F O R E V E R

Epilogue

BONY TONY

A CAUTIONARY FABLE

This is the story of Bony Tony, and this is what he looks like today.

Please understand, Tony didn't always look like that. At the start, Tony had muscles, and beautiful wavy hair, and ideas galore about what he wanted to do with his life.

For years, Tony dazzled people with his lively banter and charisma and intriguing ideas, but they started to notice that Tony never seemed to actually do anything. It didn't take people long to come to the conclusion that Tony was "all words and no action," and move on to greener pastures friend-wise, leaving -Tony confused and alone.

Tony didn't get the drift, and repeated his hopes and dreams to an empty room day after day. His mantra became, "Any minute now, things will come my way. All I have to do is wait."

In the early years, Tony waited by the mailbox, but as time went by, he embraced new technology and moved on to waiting by the telephone, then later to checking voicemail the second he walked in the door.

By the time the cell phone and texting were invented, Tony had begun to forget who he was waiting for, but he knew when they did get in touch, it would change his life for the better and make all his dreams come true.

Would it be his old girlfriend? Or maybe the company that never called back after his job interview? It might be an invitation to parties that he had heard some of his old friends were throwing, or better yet, a surprise party for him! Most certainly his older brother would see the light and finally call to apologize.

Tony became an expert at waiting. His new philosophy of life was, "Trying new things only leads to disappointment." He believed a good life would have to come to him, not the other way around.

But sadly for Tony, nothing exciting ever arrived in the mail, and nobody from the past got in touch to declare their love or apologize or offer him a job. Not a letter, not a call, and not even (gulp) an emoji.

And so, you see, there's nothing left of Tony now. Even if a call, or letter, or text did come, it's too late. It seems, though, that Tony didn't learn much from his life because the last words he ever said were— well, no one knows. He was all alone in the room at the time.

Moral of the Story: While you still have muscles on your bones, and one strand of hair somewhere on your body, and any ideas in your head, go for it, whatever "it" is for you. And do it the second you stop reading this story.

THE END or THE BEGINNING?

(you decide)

AUTHOR BIO

"I write what I live" is the motto of bestselling author and cartoonist J.J. Hubal. J.J.'s inspiring and entertaining published work spans five decades, on topics ranging from relationships to rescue animals.

J.J., together with her husband Jim, wrote Living with Your Higher Power, a recovery workbook series which has sold nearly one million copies, and *A Week at the Beach*, a guide to the life-changing power of proximity to the ocean. Her cartoons and humor essays have appeared in *Cosmopolitan*, the *Chicago Tribune*, the *Houston Post*, the HSUS magazine *Animal Sheltering*, King Features Syndicate's *Sunday Woman Plus*, and the senior health magazine *thrive,* among many others. J.J.'s cartoons were also used in two lines of greeting cards and are currently sold worldwide through Cartoon Stock.

After a lifetime of living, J.J. was hit by an avalanche of loss and disappointment that stopped her cold. Lonely and afraid, she used her unique combination of words and drawings to help her figure out what, at over seventy years of age, could possibly be next for her. The result is this hand-drawn mix of humor and hope, *Goodbye Old, Hello Bold: A Joyful Leap into a World of New Possibilities as We Age*. J.J.'s goal is to share her empowering insights and realistic ideas to give others a clear, achievable way to get past the speed bumps of life in the aging lane—and have fun doing it!

J.J. lives with Jim and their rescue cat Mango, all of whom are happily aging in place in Savannah, Georgia.

If you'd like to read more of her work, check out J.J.'s new website, jjhubal.com, or reach out via email at jjhubal@jjhubal.com.

Mango Publishing, established in 2014, publishes an eclectic list of books by diverse authors—both new and established voices—on topics ranging from business, personal growth, women's empowerment, LGBTQ studies, health, and spirituality to history, popular culture, time management, decluttering, lifestyle, mental wellness, aging, and sustainable living. We were named 2019 and 2020's #1 fastest growing independent publisher by Publishers Weekly. Our success is driven by our main goal, which is to publish high-quality books that will entertain readers as well as make a positive difference in their lives.

Our readers are our most important resource; we value your input, suggestions, and ideas. We'd love to hear from you—after all, we are publishing books for you!

Please stay in touch with us and follow us at:

Facebook: Mango Publishing
Twitter: @MangoPublishing
Instagram: @MangoPublishing
LinkedIn: Mango Publishing
Pinterest: Mango Publishing

Newsletter: mangopublishinggroup.com/newsletter

Join us on Mango's journey to reinvent publishing, one book at a time.

www.ingramcontent.com/pod-product-compliance
Lightning Source LLC
Jackson TN
JSHW031904221224
74917JS00001B/1